NO ONE YOU KNOW

BRUCE ERIC KAPLAN

Simon & Schuster

SIMON & SCHUSTER
Rockefeller Center
1230 Avenue of the Americas
New York, NY 10020

Simon & Schuster and colophon are registered trademarks of Simon & Schuster Inc.

Designed by *O'Lanso Gabbidon*

Manufactured in the United States of America
3   5   7   9   10   8   6   4   2

Library of Congress Cataloging-in-Publication Data is available.
ISBN 13: 978-1-4165-7795-9

FOREWORD

I have had a great many honors and awards in my time, and I suppose the Pulitzer Prize tops them all. Yet there are large and small moments of recognition that one gets in a lifetime that come seemingly out of the blue, and they are among the best.

They come as a major surprise because they aren't awards per se—no committees vote for them, you are not in competition with your peers—and they are seldom given to anyone you know or have worked with. Having a Broadway theater renamed the Neil Simon lit up my heart and ego with as much electricity as it took to illuminate the large letters of the theater's sign itself, located prominently on Fifty-second Street near Eighth Avenue. In that case, I was notified of the honor in advance because, much to my surprise, I had to give my permission before they would set my name in lights towering so high friends told me they could see it all the way to New Jersey (okay, just those of my friends who had telescopes as large as the one used at the Mount Wilson Observatory).

Another unexpected perk—less luminous perhaps, but just as gratifying—came recently when I was at home avidly reading *The New Yorker*, being myself not only a subscriber but a donor-subscriber, since I have given more subscriptions of *The New Yorker* to family and friends than I have donated blood during catastrophes. I think most people, upon receiving their copy of *The New Yorker*, just skim through the pages to peruse the cartoons; I know I do, mostly because they are far and away the smartest, the funniest and the best cartoons that I've ever come across. My own enjoyment of them goes back at least fifty years.

So on this one day I see a cartoon in which there is a woman (she appears to be about sixty-five and is drawn in what seems to be one continuous line—it looks as if the artist did it without ever lifting the pen from the paper, yet with no line ever crossing another) who with a defiant stance and expression says boldly to her husband (also one line from the top of his head to his toes), "If Neil Simon's going to keep writing them, we're going to keep seeing them." Clearly there will be no argument here. The husband already lost. This couple is going to that play as soon as she can call the box office.

I greatly enjoyed being the subject of the joke, the hero of the joke and the butt of the joke, because in this case it all comes out of the head—and the fingers—of a superb cartoonist, Bruce Eric Kaplan, a young man worthy of being ranked in the top echelon of *New Yorker* cartoonists, including Charles Addams, Peter Arno and the other legendary greats. Part of what makes his cartoons work so well is that if you held your hand over the drawing and read the dialogue underneath, you might think you were reading a line lifted out of any *New York Times* news report, or a statement made by a top TV news analyst, a member of the stock exchange or maybe just anyone waiting on line for a movie, a bus or a seat at the Stage Deli. The match between dialogue and drawing in Kaplan's cartoons is perfect because he makes it relatable by utilizing everyday speech, everyday clichés and every man and woman's thoughts and combining them with characters directly and simply drawn—although the one-liners are delivered more often than not by dogs, cats, fish, dinosaurs and, of course, children much older than their seven years.

Bruce Eric Kaplan is a whiz of a cartoonist, a comic writer of the first rank and a reason to look forward to each and every edition of *The New Yorker*. And now you can enjoy his work in this book as well. I did, I do and I plan to continue to.

I must go now. I hear the mailman, and I hope he has my copy of the latest *New Yorker*. Humor never takes a holiday.

Neil Simon

"I forget—did we decide to see something life-affirming or
something mind-numbing?"

"Cheese is just a substitute for the love you've never given me."

"Let's stop this before we both say a lot of things we mean."

"Where were you when I needed an imaginary friend?"

"Woulda, coulda, shoulda. Next!"

"No one tells you how difficult the transition is from colorful eccentric to out-of-control crackpot."

"*I don't know if this is how I'm meant to be wasting my education.*"

"A day is a long time."

"There are two kinds of people. You're not one of them."

"Let's cut the exposition and get straight to the sex."

"After fifteen years of therapy, I still don't know why I crossed the road."

"I heard it through the grape jam."

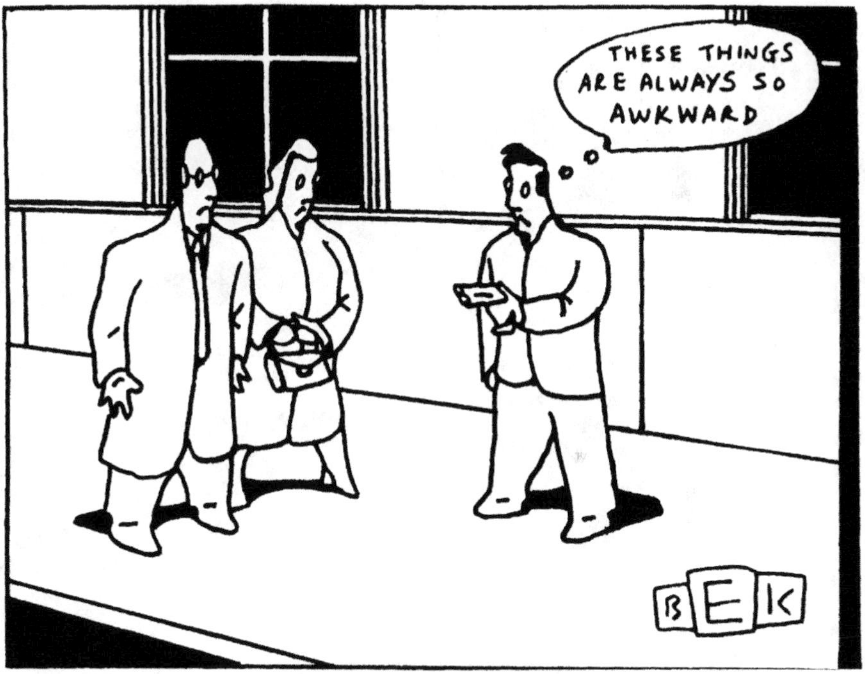
THESE THINGS ARE ALWAYS SO AWKWARD
BEK

"I'm tired of playing by the rules. Let's scratch their eyes out till they give us fresh tuna."

"It's a jungle gym out there."

"*So you think I should just ignore it?*"

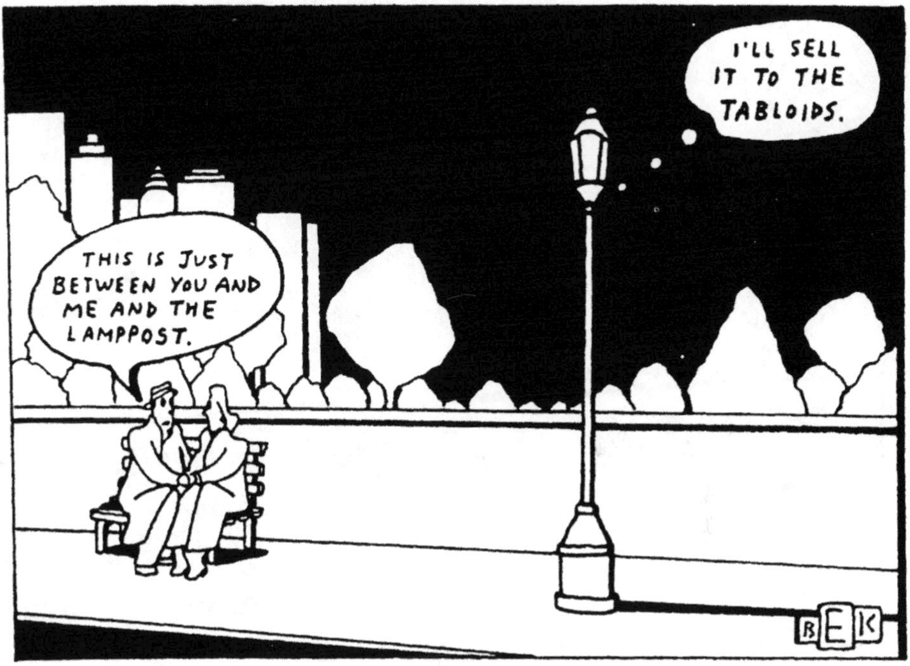
THIS IS JUST BETWEEN YOU AND ME AND THE LAMPPOST.
I'LL SELL IT TO THE TABLOIDS.
BEK

"You heard me. This is it. We had a three-picture deal."

"Well, according to the scuttlebutt we're dead."

"I'm sorry. I just feel I should be dating someone closer to my daughter's age."

"Did you ever have one of those days when you felt you would never be soft and fluffy again?"

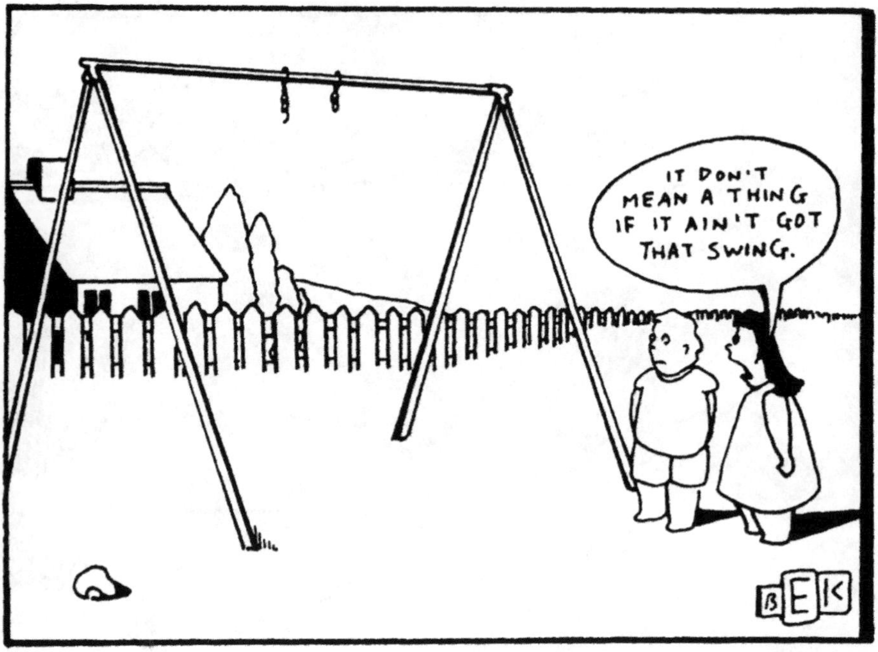
IT DON'T MEAN A THING IF IT AIN'T GOT THAT SWING.
BEK

"*Well, I do have this recurring dream that one day I might see some results.*"

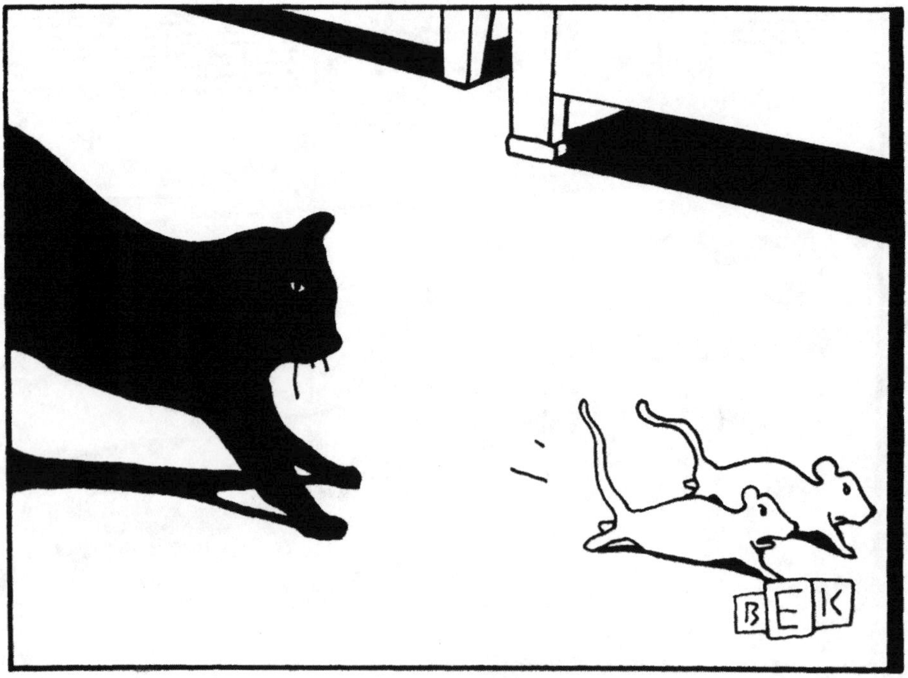
BEK

"The system sucks."

"Listen, Mom, I'm not your little girl anymore."

"See? Isn't this better than being happy?"

"Who ever told you you could sing?"

"*Someday, you'll act like you understand.*"

"I appreciate the fact that you're trying to do something different. Now cut it out."

"Tonight's performance has been canceled because the star of our show has decided that musicals are stupid."

"*Maybe I'm just old-fashioned, but I think you should keep everything bottled up inside you.*"

"Of course I understand it. It's just some Grisham potboiler."

"Do you want to get out of here and grab a cup of coffee?"

"I told him he's got to learn to let go."

"It is a tale told by an idiot, full of sound and fury, signifying nothing, and number one on the best-seller list."

"*So I brought a little work home with me. Big deal.*"

"You're using the boogeyman as an excuse to shut me out."

Obviously, they had too many refrigerator magnets.

"Just do the work. No one cares if you get goose bumps."

"I've seen it performed many times, but I can't remember ever sleeping through it so peacefully."

"I may *want to sit. Just give me a chance to process this.*"

"I had a wonderful time. Now if you'll excuse me, I have to go home and second-guess my feelings for you."

"*I* bought *the roses. I don't need to smell them.*"

"*Now, be careful. Some of them try to pass as geniuses when really they're just bad dressers.*"

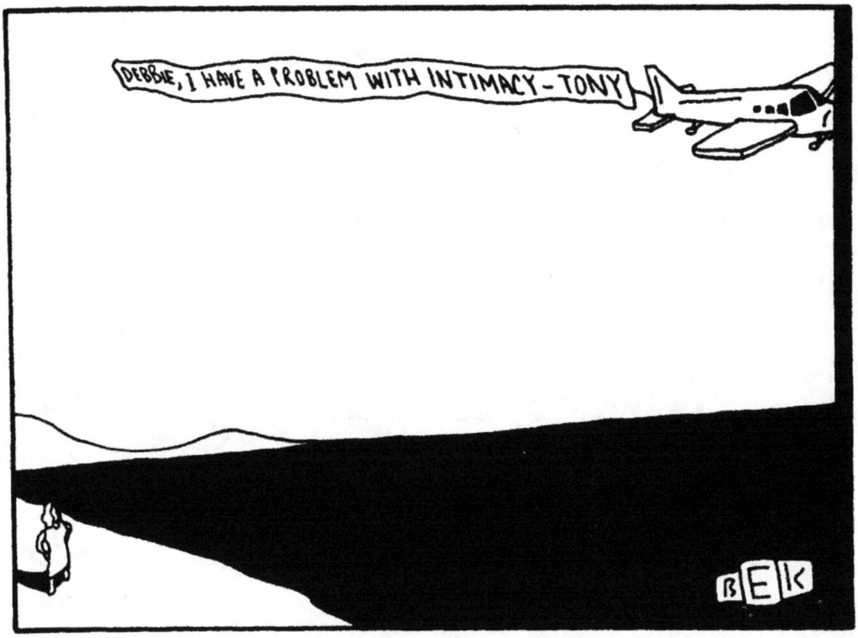
DEBBIE, I HAVE A PROBLEM WITH INTIMACY - TONY
BEK

"So—Helen tells me you're dead."

"It was so depressing. When I go to the theater, I want to be entertained."

"I've been getting a lot of peace and quiet. Except in my head, of course."

"We, the jury, find the defendant guilty of killing her softly with his song."

"Wouldn't you know—the one time I fall in love with a bunny he turns out to be chocolate."

"Sometimes it's as if I didn't know the difference between what's real and what's trompe l'oeil."

"How do you work one of these?"

"I'll be home in a bit. Would you mind slapping together some kind of relationship?"

"*There are plenty of other women who would kill to feel lonely with me.*"

"*Why does* he *always get to be the boy?*"

"We keep this section closed off."

"I find that incessant barking eases the pain."

"He's actually quite bright for someone who went to Harvard."

"*I don't have any easy answers for you. I do know that I find Dr. Seuss can sometimes be a source of comfort.*"

"I'm going crazy staring at the same four legs."

"My back is fine. My mind went out."

"It's not that we don't appreciate the attention. We just feel that it
would be healthier for you to focus on something other than us."

"We finally heard from your bearings. They're never coming back."

"Well, it works for Susan Sontag."

"Things are crazy right now. Let me get back to you after the holidays."

"I'd appreciate it if you talked to me without staring at my gills."

"*Take away his brilliant prose and he's just some depressed guy.*"

"Why ask for the stars? We have the moon."

"*I need an ensemble film. Take five star vehicles and smush them together.*"

"Let's drive up to New England and watch the leaves die."

"*They never change. It's just that as we get older we develop a higher tolerance for dorks.*"

"*I want you to leave and take your headlong slide into oblivion with you.*"

"I don't know what being a sweater is like, but it's got to be better than this."

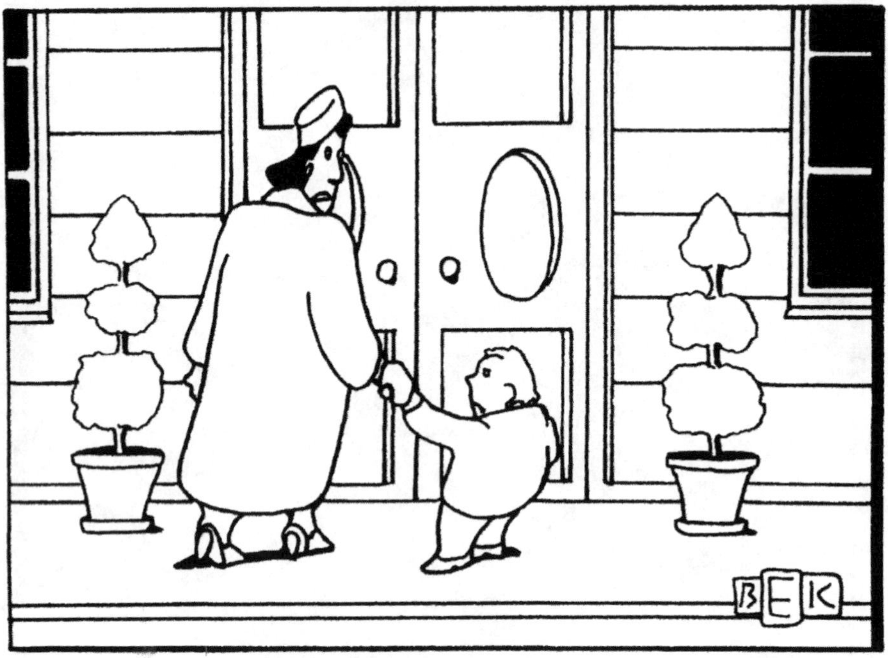
BEK

"Now, remember, act cute."

"If music be the food of love, shut up."

"*I want you to have this. It belonged to my mother.*"

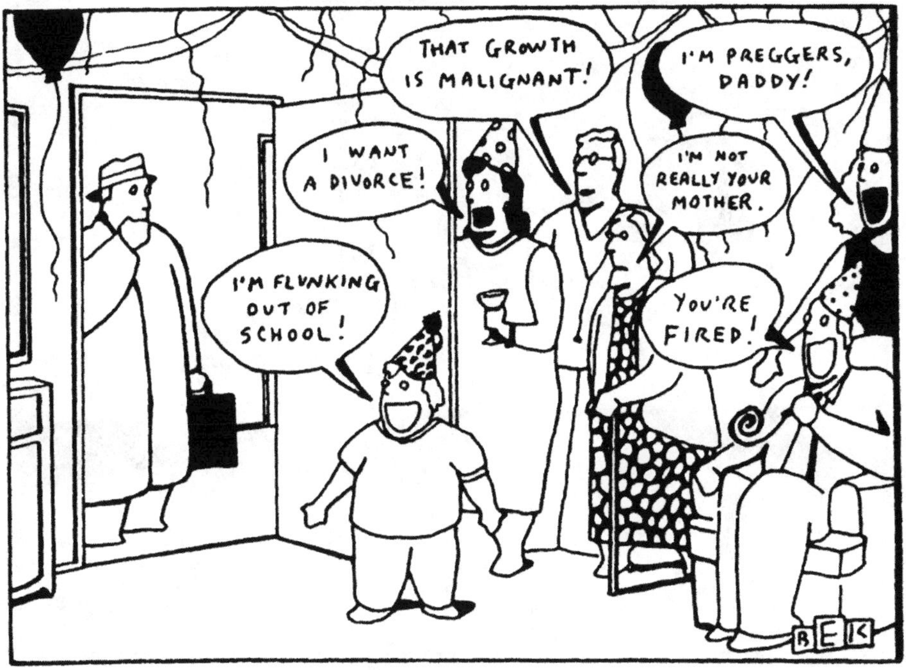
THAT GROWTH IS MALIGNANT!
I'M PREGGERS, DADDY!
I WANT A DIVORCE!
I'M NOT REALLY YOUR MOTHER.
I'M FLUNKING OUT OF SCHOOL!
YOU'RE FIRED!
BEK

Surprise Party

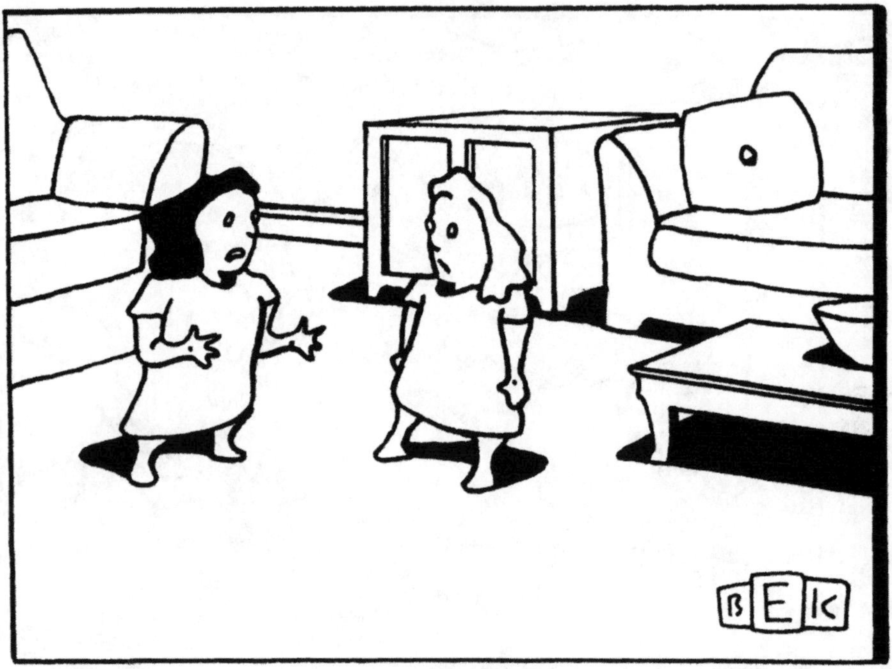
BEK

"All he did was stick gum in my hair, and now I have to put up with all this innuendo."

"No, last year he went to summer camp. This year he went to prison."

"*I think I'm finally getting over this silly fear of abandonment.*"

"Maybe I could have done more with myself if I hadn't been so focused on tearing up the sofa."

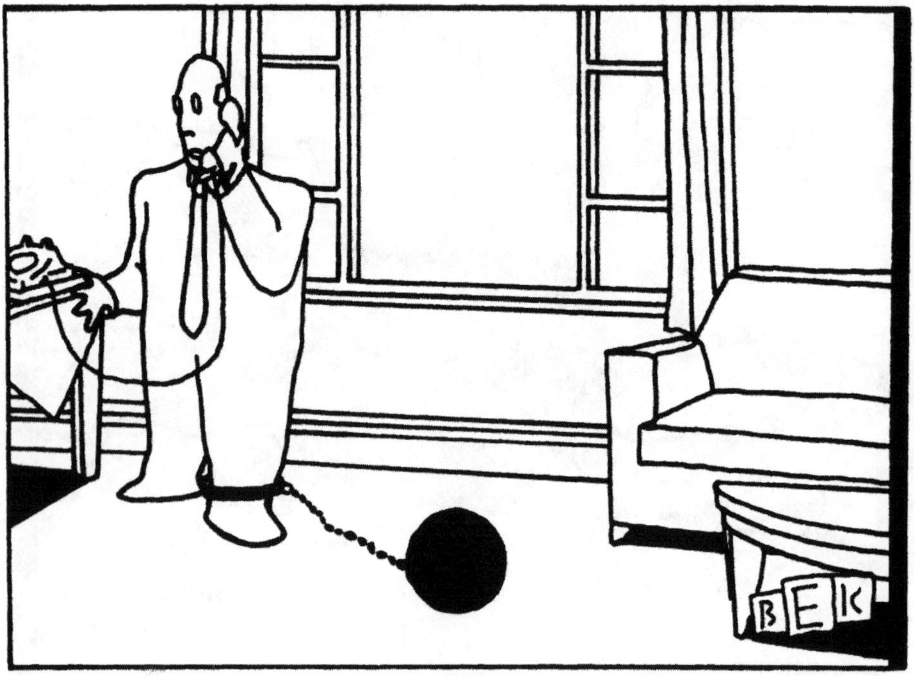
BEK

"It was her dying wish."

"Location, location, location."

"An elephant never forgets."

"*I want to be saved, but at the same time I want to be spent.*"

"Call me shallow—I like Goodnight Moon."

"*This summer, we decided to stay home and complain.*"

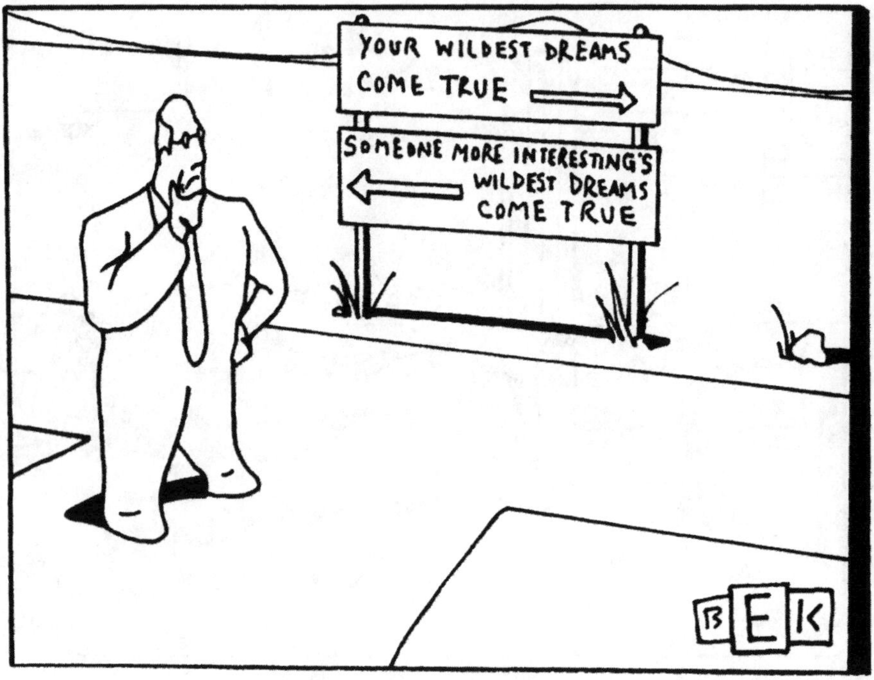
YOUR WILDEST DREAMS COME TRUE
SOMEONE MORE INTERESTING'S WILDEST DREAMS COME TRUE
BEK

"*I sleep half the year—how much more space do you need?*"

"He feels life is too precious to actually do anything."

"*Darling, trust me. Santa isn't going to give you a network.*"

" 'Pee on the carpet!' That's your solution to everything."

"Stop referring to you and me as 'we'!"

"Gee, you're not at all like your obituaries."

"Wait! Come back! I was just kidding about wanting to be happy."

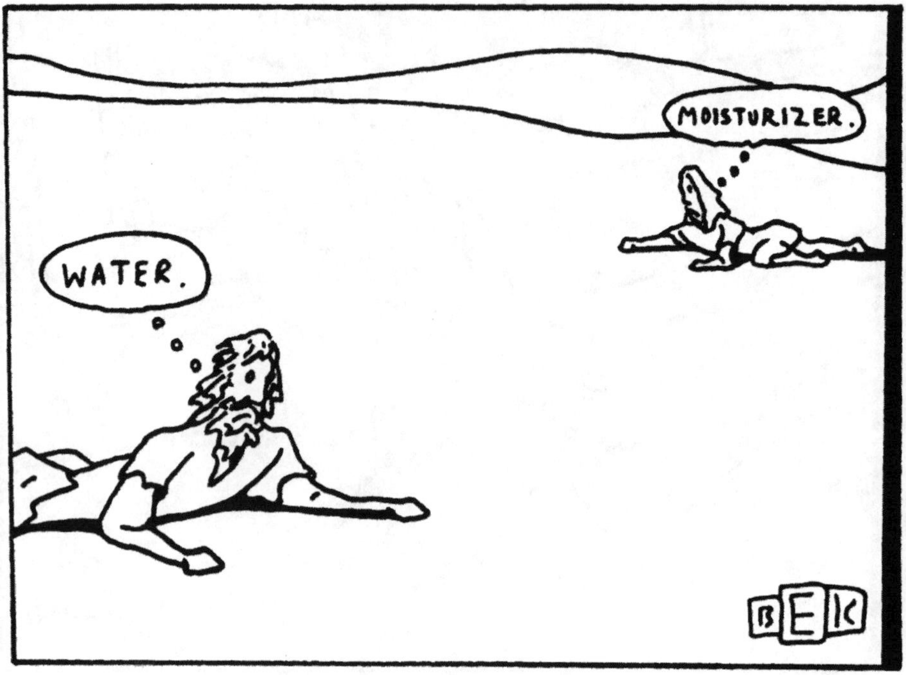
MOISTURIZER.
WATER.
BEK

"For heaven's sake, Melissa, she's my mother. I can't tell
her to leave."

"You look as if you don't expect fireworks, you act as if you don't expect fireworks, you say you don't expect fireworks. But something tells me you expect fireworks."

"Sweet? I thought you wanted someone with edge."

"I'll be straight with you. I was put on this planet to make your life miserable."

"If only he had gone into the white light and stayed there."

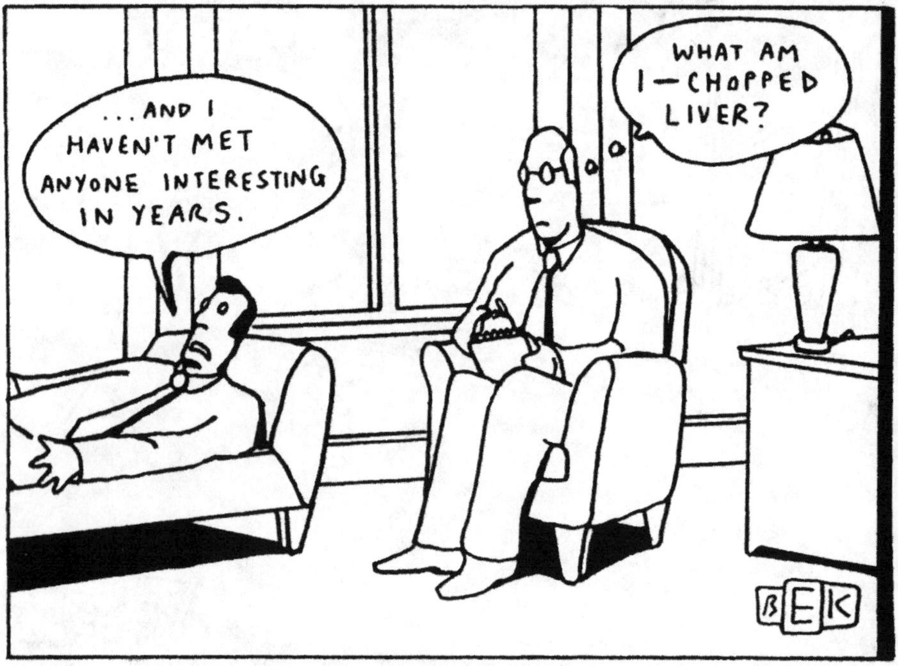
...AND I HAVEN'T MET ANYONE INTERESTING IN YEARS.
WHAT AM I—CHOPPED LIVER?
BEK

"*I don't just want to write. I want to be in literary feuds.*"

"Don't get me wrong—I loved Schindler's List. *I just think* Jaws
was a much better film."

"Oh, sure, I remember him. He was quiet, mostly kept to himself, paid the rent on time. You know, we were only married for sixteen years."

"*Okay, I feel complete. Now what?*"

"I'm only flesh and blood. And, of course, collagen."

"Under 'Occupation' I usually just put 'Roam the earth.'"

"How do you think I feel when you say those years in the jungle were the happiest time of your life?"

"Not only has everything been said, but I have absolutely no idea who said any of it."

"*I have so much I want to express, but when I try to put it into Play-Doh it never comes out right.*"

"*I need a change. Normally, I just wear the faint odor of vague discomfort and unhappiness.*"

"Since we're both being honest, I should tell you I have fleas."

"When will I be old enough to start suing people?"

"Will you be going by the market?"

"*It's a moment of clarity. It'll pass.*"

"Mostly I'm driven by my fear of not eating enough people."

"Why did you speak to Dad? He can't green-light anything."

"All in all, I could have done with a little less good, clean living."

"No, this is crazy. We mustn't."

"*Damn it, agree to whatever she demands. No matter what it takes, I want my mommy.*"

"If Neil Simon's going to keep writing them, we're going to keep seeing them."

"*Tell her she's dead. I don't want to talk about the relationship.*"

"*When I bought him, I went for craftsmanship. Now I wish I had gone for snuggliness.*"

"*Can you spare a few seconds to minimize my problems?*"

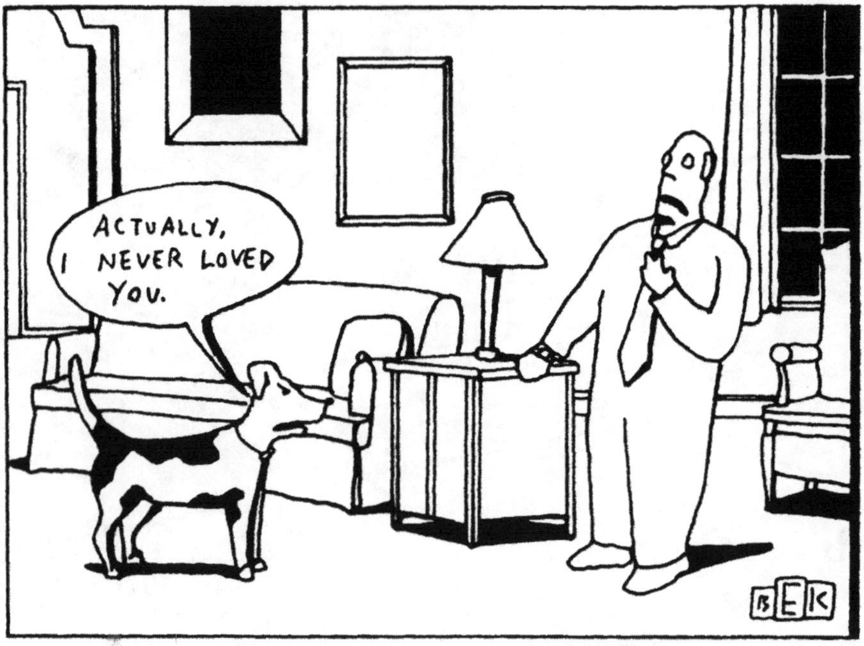
ACTUALLY, I NEVER LOVED YOU.
BEK

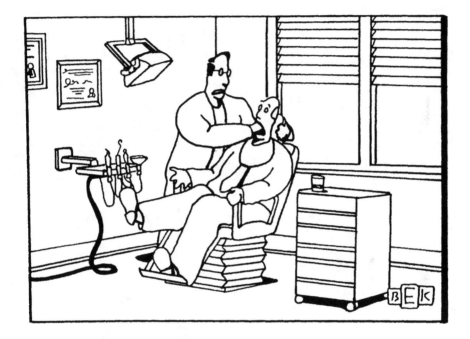

"Gee, this is like pulling teeth."

"Nice try, Mom, but I'm going to go with a caterer."

"After five hundred pages, I wish this jerk would come of age already."

"What if my child-eating years are over?"

"You never said anything about having your own life."

"*I stepped back and looked at the big picture. I wasn't in it.*"

"*I find it very significant that you would rather play house.*"

"I've always had this dream of buying a little farm and then
selling it off piece by piece."

"Everything is so easy for you."

"I want the whole thing gutted."

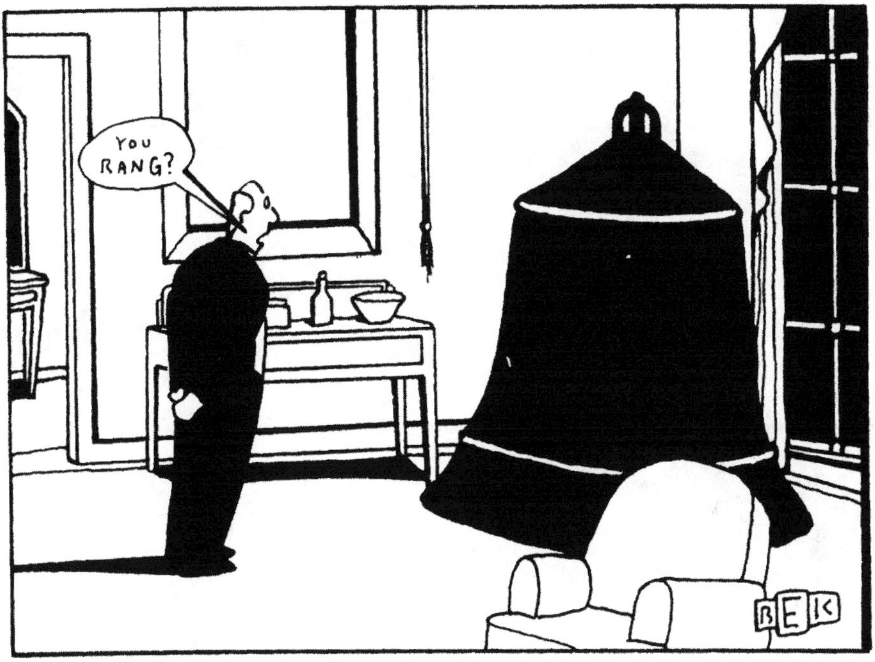
YOU RANG?
BEK

"*Oh, that reminds me. We need a new dishwasher.*"

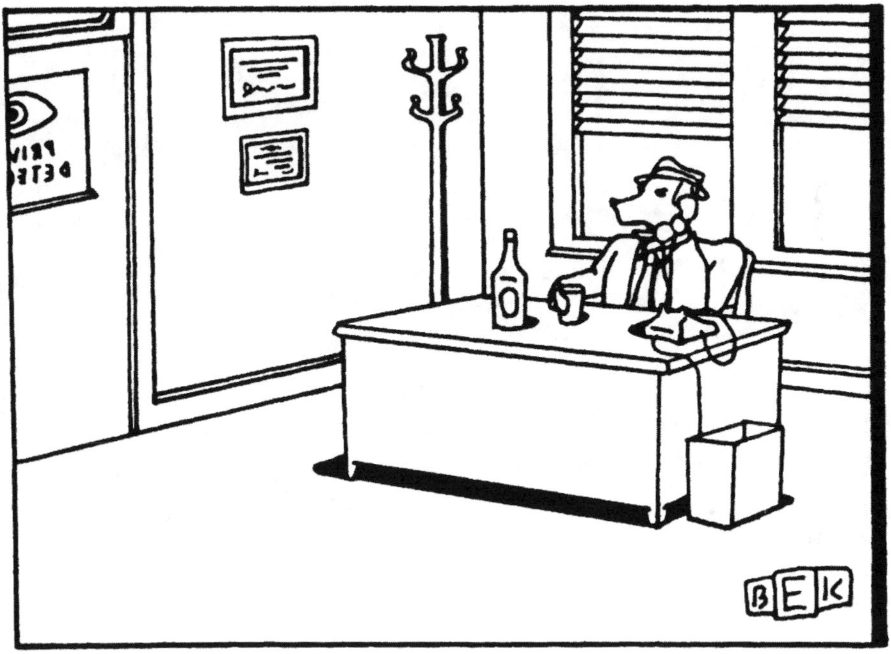
BEK

"Fetch it yourself."

"And then, as soon as I had carved out my niche, they went and had another kid."

"Too much agony, not enough ecstasy."

"At least he grunts. The last one didn't even try to communicate."

"I know the truth would set me free, but who wants to go out there?"

"*I don't have the heart to tell him what's going on with today's art market.*"

"You can't let all the power and fame make you lose sight of that naive, innocent kid who was in it just for the money."

"*I think, therefore I'm tired.*"

"I see, your name is Dad. And what family did you say you're with?"

"People are okay, but I prefer little pieces of string."

"My problem is I grew up on cartoons, thinking that's what real life would be like."

"*You have to admit he provides a nice counterbalance to the room's slightly sterile quality.*"

"Now, according to this agreement, his problems will be your problems, and your problems will be your problems."

"*I understand completely. I like good movies, and you like bad movies.*"

"Right now, I'm between naps."

"I'm trying to change the subject, but you keep telling me how you feel."

"I've already made arrangements to be flushed down the toilet."

"I'm sick of writing book reports on spec."

"Who cares if it's crap? It's digitally enhanced."

"Keep in mind that these are my friends. You're just a prop."

"There, there—it was only a dream. There's no such thing as people."

"Of all the finger-painting classes in all the day-care centers in all the world, you had to walk into mine."

"Let your precious e-mail get you out of this one."

"Well, there's no sense in us both getting a lobotomy."

"It's such a nice day. Why don't you go outside and make some money?"

"I don't care if it's a boy or a girl, just as long as I'm healthy."

"This isn't tap water, is it?"

"I used to be innocent. Then I was naive. Now I'm just dumb."

"Apparently, back in Transylvania, he was a big deal."

"Before kindergarten, I was into that whole downtown nursery-school scene."

"It's hard to be process oriented, what with all this focus on treats."

"I know. But I think I can change him."

"I'm sorry, but the flight of the bumblebees has been canceled."

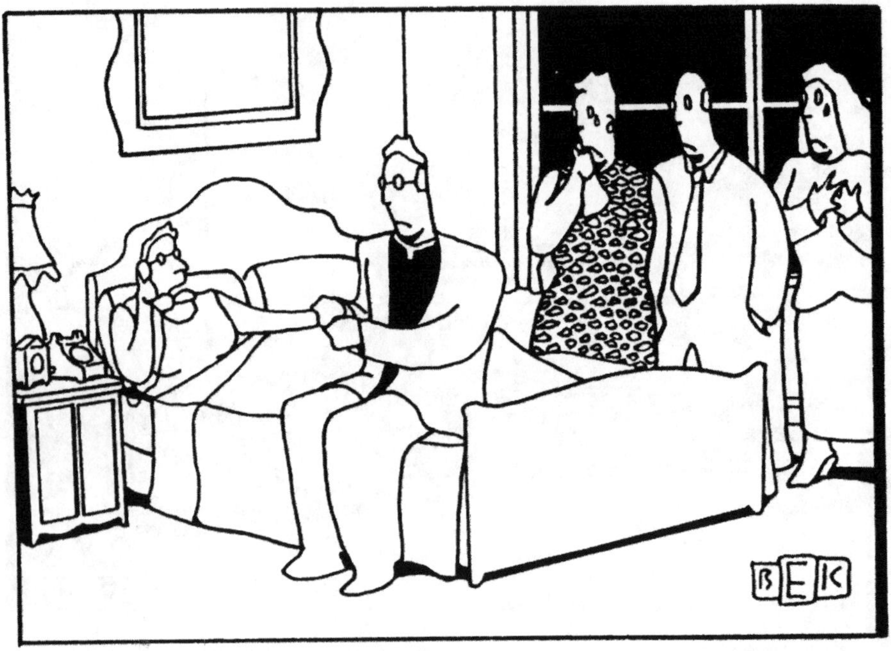
BEK

"Look, I'm dying. Gotta go."

"I'm a wunderkind slash flop."

"*I try to listen to that little voice inside me, but it's always boring me with the details.*"

"This is nothing personal. It's just school."

"In case you hadn't noticed, I stopped being your kumquat years ago.

"*I feel bad about this on an intellectual level, but I'm hungry.*"

"Why don't you just say it? You think I do nothing all day."

*"I don't have time to talk about this now. Can't it wait
until we're dead?"*

"I had a childhood, too, but you don't see me writing about it."

"I'm sorry, but you know too much."

Printed in the United States
By Bookmasters